A DEMOCRACY OF POETS

AGS PUBLISHING, CARBONDALE, COLORADO

A DEMOCRACY OF POETS

**POEMS OF
THE ROARING FORK VALLEY
AND BEYOND**

EDITED BY

KIM NUZZO | MARJORIE DELUCA | CAMERON SCOTT | RETT HARPER

ISBN: 978-0-9847972-3-3

Some poems in this anthology have been previously published. Publishing information received from authors are at the end of each poem, and are reproduced as submitted by the author.

Cover and text design and production by AGS Publishing
Cover photograph: Florence, Italy, by Marjorie DeLuca

AGS Publishing
a division of Aspen Graphic Solutions
947 Vitos Way · Carbondale, Colorado 81623
info@aspengfx.com

CONTENTS

Cameron Scott

We are here. We are here in the push and jumble, flash and glitz, non-profit, for profit, for our sanity and yours, ski-valley bumming, river hopping, natural resource extracting, mountain absorbing, peach growing, heart unfolding, land.

Land of entitlement and wealth. Land of solitude just around the corner. Land of discovering deeply. Land of the up-valley commute. This is the land we fell in love with before everything changed. This land is land still changing. This is the land that collects red dust and insect wings carried in from the desert. This is our land.

Like many of us, I arrived in this land adrift. A Colorado native returned to the dusty west in search of a poetic center, a place where I did not have to live in a big city to be immersed in poetry, a place I did not have to sit forever on the outskirts and edges looking in, a place where language was alive and teeming with life.

Because of a collective poetry gathering at Town Center Booksellers, because of finding a poem in the local paper describing bottom-barrel wages for an immigrant landscaper trying to support a family, because of a monthly poetry reading in Aspen at Zélé Café with host Kim Nuzzo, I stayed.

It is hard to tell what the arc and length of something might be. Town Center Booksellers closed. Poets, beautiful poets, mad poets, spiritual, wholesome, jazzy, no-holds-barred poets have birthed themselves, all because a poem published in the local paper sparked the creation of a practicing poetry collective.

In the interim, a revered local poet, all guts and intellect and spirit, passed away, and our grief was turned into an annual poetry festival at Thunder

River Theatre Company in memory and celebration.

Open mic venues have sprung up all across the Roaring Fork Valley. The Blend, Steve's Guitars and PAC3 in Carbondale. Victoria's Espresso in Aspen. Large non-profits like the Aspen Writers' Foundation have begun bringing poets, slam poets, poets of magical intent, into our schools.

And finally, that monthly poetry reading in Aspen, the one hosted by Kim Nuzzo that has quietly and steadily provided a venue for poets to gather, year after year, through snow and rain and sunshine, across passes and up canyons, to listen to music, each other, and a featured poet from somewhere along the Western Slope and beyond, continues.

PREFACE

Kim Nuzzo & Cameron Scott

The Aspen Poets' Society—a diverse democracy of poets on the Western Slope of Colorado. Grocery clerks, teachers, transplants, musicians, miners, counselors, students, designers, housewives, fishing guides and librarians, backwoods squatters, dancers and trust funders, or as Walt Whitman might have said, a piece of "America singing."

These poets gather in a variety of venues to honor the word, speak and share the word with each other and with whomever will listen. This democracy of poetry welcomes all forms of poetry.

This anthology represents as many of these voices as we could solicit from poets who have in one way or another participated in this west-of-the–Continental Divide chorus, at that monthly poetry reading in Aspen that has kept pace with the changing years.

We expect you will find the same variety of genres as you find types of music on your satellite radio: blues, country, metal, punk, folk, classic, rap and many more. Poetry is everywhere in this land, in everyone, whether they realize it or not.

We are confident you will find poems here that speak to you. Praise the artists, praise the art form, praise that thing just out of reach, just around the corner.

Welcome to a piece of America singing.

A DEMOCRACY OF POETS

Karen Glenn

A GOOD DAY

My mother was a beauty
and dressed it. One Sunday
the preacher quipped,
"Even Solomon in all his glory
was not arrayed like one of these."

Now she's 76. Thin and hairless,
she wears a cheap wig, dirty tennis shoes.
She sees poorly, drives worse.
One Monday, she hits a parked car
in the cancer patient lot. Muddled,
she just drives away. A day later,
police call. Somebody caught
her license plate number.

I'm surprised she tells this story on herself.
It's not her way. Then I hear that old tone
in her voice. "The witness described me
as an attractive blond," she says,
"in her fifties."

"A Good Day" was originally published in the Portland Review.

José Alcantara

ORISON

Upon your head a pox
of yellow swallowtails.

Upon your tongue a plague
of purple peonies.

May rainbows ravage
your summer skies,
raspberries run riot
and nightingales never stop.

May the moon drop silver coins
upon your toes
and the lust of lilacs
ravish your sleep.

May the hooting of owls
plant marigolds in your ears.

May you drown in the cloud-
shattered rain of hallelujah.

First published in Every Day Poets.

Richard Newman

BLESS THEIR HEARTS

At Steak-n-Shake I learned that if you add
"Bless their hearts" after their names, you can say
whatever you want about them and it's OK.
My son, bless his heart, is an idiot,
she said. He rents storage space for his kids'
toys—they're only one and three years old!
I said, my father, bless his heart, has turned
into a sentimental old fool. He gets
weepy when he hears my daughter's greeting
on our voice mail. Before our Steakburgers came
someone else blessed her officemate's heart,
then, as an afterthought, the jealous hearts
of the entire anthropology department.
We bestowed blessings on many a heart
that day. I even blessed my ex-wife's heart.
Our waiter, bless his heart, would not be getting
much tip, for which, no doubt, he'd bless our hearts.
In a week it would be Thanksgiving,
and we would each sit with our respective
families, counting our blessings and blessing
the hearts of family members as only family
does best. Oh, bless us all, yes, bless us, please
bless us and bless our crummy little hearts.

From Domestic Fugues (*Steel Toe Books, 2009*). *Originally appeared in* Crab Orchard Review, *Winter/Spring 2007*)

Jan Hadwen Hubbell

POCKET POET

Let me be your pocket poet
And steal away on your hip
To Norway
Where we'll live in a tiny
Farmhouse that smells of
Lambs and old wood.
I'll fry you up a
Sonnet for breakfast made fresh
From the lilacs breathing
Through the open window.
Put me in the reed basket
Of your rusty bike
And I'll sing childish ballads as
You pedal to the fiord for fish.
The breeze will blow syncopated
Rhymes through your gentle hair
And your weathered lips will
Whisper the grace of waterfall's
purpose in return.

For your own pocket poet
Will mark the sweetness of
Every scent, the joy in every
Breeze, the sight of the rolling
Sea and the hills that scream with green.

At night when you rest
On the old farm's horse hair
Mattress, and pull the dizzying quilt
Up to our chins,
And the lambs peek in the half open

Window, parted black casements
The way your lips parted for
This stowaway who brings
The steady colors of secret
Love into your wailing heart.

José Alcantara

THERE WAS A COUP TODAY
IN PARAGUAY

and the hummingbirds are sticking out their tongues
and the guanacos are gathering their spit

and the peccaries are throwing off their collars
and the ocelots are sharpening their claws

and the tapirs' lips are all in a snarl
and the howler monkeys are starting to howl

and everyone is more or less alarmed
than the capybara

who sleeps with only his nose above water
in spite of the disgusting stench.

First published in The New Verse News.

Kathleen Maris

AM IS THE ROOT OF LOVE

I hunch at the end of the bed.
He sits on the portable toilet.
With clenched teeth, You don't understand!

I face my back to him.
I can't catch you if you fall.

I'm finished, he says.

I turn,
hand him some tissue.

He shrugs his shoulders,
gives me a half wink.

I help him to bed,
take out the removable pan
and clean it.

Roger Adams

OUT ON A WEEKEND

It was in Nogales
then led straight to hell
I was out on a weekend
when she told me it was now or never

Wake up to the smell my friend
wake up to your own set of peanuts
know that memories
are the stuff you put up your nose

They are the things your mother showed you
those bits of wisdom
your children revealed
while just being little kids

No one call tell you anything she told me
the only voice you hear is yours
your dad sleeps up there
under a flag they keep replacing

Listen to the words
of the song he sings in Spanish
spell check gets it wrong every time
"No es tu vida que vives"

It's not your life you live
in Nogales it's true of everyone
get out now while you still can
the woman won't wait too long

The ball will go where you look

glance back but don't stare
it's only a moment
take a snapshot and one to share

break all your mirrors
drive straight ahead
you're out on a weekend
and nobody really cares

Rosemerry Wahtola Trommer

EIGHT LOST AND FOUNDS

one cold night
everything gold
is brown

where, I say, is the bliss?
nowhere, says Ulli, until
it's inside of you

lost: a car key,
a credit card, a friend's coat,
my certainty

two untied balloons
one glorious
sky

humming a tune
about October, how it goes,
October goes

brown, brown, brown, brown, brown,
countless unnamed shades
of (oh!) brown

found: another question,
a car key, a credit card,
a friend's coat, a loss

to the one missing it
that much sweeter
the scent of rain

Previously published in Living the Life: Tales from America's Mountains and Ski Towns,
by David J. Rothman. Denver, Colorado: Conundrum Press, 2013.

Karen Glenn
KOREA

My father is sleeping in that tent again,
where every night the rats still run and run
across his body, and every night
he still slaps them—hard—away from him,
never waking, never knowing
that it's my mother's hand, soft
against his chest, reaching
for him in the dark.

Korea was originally published in the Lullwater Review.

Craig Nielson

COME BACK TO US
EVERETT RUESS

Oh Everett
wanderer of wilderness before wilderness
seeker and maker of the inscrutable mystery
in the time before highways
you, your small dog and burros
probing those immeasurable broken canyons
and wrinkled geologic mesas
with your open artist heart
pack full of canvas and poems
needless of anything more
than that Kismet of wildness
under those yawning desert skies
rotten with light and stars
leaving us the way you did
forsaken
and wanting you to remain missing
and never found to this maddening world
walking off with your fair smile
filled as you were
with all that barren beauty
into the red abyss

Kim Nuzzo

THE SAYINGS OF
TWILIGHT JESUS

Twilight is busy during the day and doesn't eat properly. Driving, at times he becomes disoriented and has trouble seeing, double images, momentarily.

"I'm a walk-in. One who just steps into the wound rather than from birth. There is no place to hide. You want the keys of the kingdom? They're staring you right in the face. If only I could split heaven with a knife, spill its seeds out like a blizzard of miracles. Perhaps it starts with the ravens. I listen to Cobain. All the puppets are lost."

Art Goodtimes
AFTER LI PO

The birds

have long lifted up
as a flock & flown

Only a lonely cloud floats by

the two of us
lost in our looking

the mountain & I

Previously published in the Telluride Watch *and the* Four Corners Free Press *(Cortez).*

Cam Scott

PILGRIMAGE

After dark, driving blind and drifting on 82
as Mt. Sopris shifts positions, clouds shift,
the river grade rises and wraps around corners.
I am a body in motion, the first one toward heaven.
I am a body at rest, a second palming of death.
A seat within a seat, closest to weary, cousin
to the midnight bus, vehicles nod in succession.
The snow that blows sideways, sticks sideways.
The river that falls like a silver fish in the snow,
road sign to the soul, finds a path home each night
as the canyon opens up and swallows it whole.

David Romtvedt

BIRDS SINGING
FOR JESUS

Jesus was a carpenter,
but it's hard to picture him
hiding nails—mornings at work,
then sharing a sandwich, a coarse joke,
later walking to the olive grove
to take a leak.

He was also a preacher
whose gaze and cool tone
made his listeners long to touch him.
But he was so famously indifferent to sex
that it seems pornographic to picture him
in bed with a wife, his leg thrown over hers,
much less an erection.

It's easier to speak of the bitter fruit
of paternity, that crown of thorns.
And what would it feel like to be the one
human only half born of humanity?

When Jesus hung on the cross,
there was little for the Roman Guards to do.
They put down their spears and pulled off
their helmets. They cut slivers of wood
to clean their teeth, pitched coins at a rock
and bet on which would land closest,
kicked a wad of rags around in the dust
and, lifting their arms above their heads,
yelled goal. At sunset, they lowered
the dead man to earth.

Here we are then—strange and ordinary—
climbing down from our crosses
to drive trucks or repair TVs,
to cut meat or harvest soybeans.

Today I got a letter from my father
who died in 1950, two weeks
before I was born. The postman
explained nothing. My father said
his greatest regret was
that we would never meet.

He'd already started writing
when a nurse said, "The rain's stopped.
Wouldn't you like to look out the window?"
She propped him up with pillows and he saw
the sun on the metal surfaces of the cars,
on the galvanized blades of the rooftop ventilators,
and on a puddle where a flock of sparrows
was bathing. They flapped their wings
and the water flew up, refracting the light.
"Those birds," he wrote, "were singing away
like they were giving a concert
even if I was the only person who'd come."

There's no letter. I was an adult
when my father died an unhappy
not quite old man. He was a carpenter,
but I don't believe he could have worked on a crew
with Jesus. He could hardly work with anyone.
Still, I wanted to have another chance.
I wanted those birds to be singing for him.

First published in Narrative Magazine.

Lawton Eddy

DRIVEN TO BEAUTY

Some mornings
small actions are my saviors

raising the shade
running water into a glass
fastening the tiny clasp on a bracelet

so simple, yet somehow— marvelous

Now
when such enormous action is needed
it's curious I am content with these

You see, since that election
when the blue and red got so mixed up
my country turned into a huge purple bruise
and we stared at each other
despair and disbelief taking turns distorting our faces

my attention to the tangy hit of an orange slice on my tongue
has magnified

You see, I just don't hear it any more
the political clamor and the horrible truths
my mental factory has just stopped
manufacturing plans—for the revolution

instead, I paint my walls in daring colors, stand longer in front of art,
laugh loudly at jokes. Dance more.

Sitting with my pen

all I can do is write poems about beauty

Perhaps, by sheer contrast
this retaliatory tumble into joy
is the most utterly subversive thing of all

Previously published in the chapbook, On Stage: River City Nomads, Poetry Performances Volume One 2004–2009

David Rothman

ELEGANT SNOWFLAKE:
A HAIKU SEQUENCE

The Art of Snow Viewing: An Intuitive View of Snow. Snow and ava-
lanches, like all wonders of Nature, reveal themselves on micro and
macro levels. Japanese artists, especially many of the ancient haiku
poets, lived much of their lives in snow. By reading their poems one can
begin to understand that the snow flake is much more than frozen
water falling from the sky. We will explore these complex and elegant
forms, the forces in our atmosphere and imagination which constantly
drive this dynamic system. Along the way, we'll contemplate the poetry
and metaphorical power of snow, and how mountain communities co-
exist with and pay tribute to its destructive manifestation. No previous
experience with snow, skiing or avalanche awareness is required.

— Advertisement for a poetry writing workshop

1.

The snow is falling.
I am really fucking drunk.
Why am I naked?

The snow is on me.
I am in a snow bank now.
It is very cold.

Beautiful snowflake,
Why are you stuck in my eye?
Fuck off, you snowflake.

In Colorado,
We think snow is beautiful.
We like vodka, too.
I need a blanket.

Where are the apartment keys?
I'd like a drink now.

Cherry blossom? What
Cherry blossom. I don't see
A cherry blossom.

Elegant snowflakes,
I can write my name in you
Like this: wee, wee, wee.

2 .

Excuse me, mister.
Could you please help me to break
This stupid window?

Thanks, I'm ok, man.
It's my apartment. No keys.
That? It's my beacon.

I am wearing it
In case snow falls off that roof.
Look…batteries good.

No, most people don't
Wear avalanche beacons and
No shoes. Or clothing.

Did I tell you that
My girlfriend moved out today?
Hey, thanks for the ride.

Those flashing lights on
Your car are really cool, dude.
I don't have ID.

Still snowing. You know,
Snowflakes are more than
Frozen water. Shit.

3 .

Why are you laughing?
Is it something that I said?
Her name is Ashley.

She left this bottle
Of vodka and so I drank
All of it. So there.

These clothes don't fit right.
Orange is not my color.
Sorry I threw up.

You guys are funny.
This bed is too hard for me.
But warmer than snow.

Do you like the snow?
I like skiing in the snow.
Let's all go skiing.

Ashley has great tits,
But sometimes she is so mean.
I'm getting sleepy.

Here is my beacon.
I think we can turn it off.
See you for breakfast.

Do me a favor?
Would one of you call Ashley,
And tell her that I

Drank all the vodka,
But that her cat is inside
And I forgive her

Because she is like
Snow, a wonder of nature,
That falls from the sky.

Previously published in the book Living the Life: Tales from America's Mountains and Ski Towns, *by David J. Rothman. Denver, Colorado: Conundrum Press, 2013.*

Laurie James

ONION THIEF

A woman I saw yesterday
had small crooked hands that clutched
at her coat to keep the cold out.
Her head was coiled in scarves,
like snakes ready to strike.
I watched as she chose
one small white onion from the bin
and dropped it into her bag.
Her eyes were lowered as she walked away.

A thief of onions right here.
I did nothing, but turned to the stack
of apples, thinking all the while of the
white onion resting in the bottom of her bag—
its layers circling around itself;
its fate, a frying pan with cheap
melted margarine; the smell permeating
her small space where her breath
fouls the air as she sleeps.
I could be that woman.
Hungry for the pungent bulb—
its sweetness
all there is.

David Mason

HORSE PEOPLE

When Quanah Parker's mother as a young girl
saw her family lanced and hacked to pieces,
and was herself thrown on the hurtling rump
of a warrior's pony whipped to the far off
and utterly unwritten Comancheria,
the little blond began her life, outcast
only when the whites recaptured her and killed
the man she loved, the father of her children.

The language she forgot would call her ruined
and beyond redemption like the young she suckled,
among them the "last Chief of the Comanche,"
a man who died in comforts his mother spurned,
but who, like her, remembered how the manes
of the remuda caught the breezes as they ran,
and how the grass caught fire in the scalp-red sun.

First published in The Southwest Review.

Catherine Garland

CHILDHOOD DREAMS

Parachinar, Punjab, the Hindu Kush—
Deliciously the words roll in my mouth,
And melt like butter curls and memories.

Early mornings, before the midday heat,
My mother sat with me under a chinar tree
And taught me how to read the newspaper,
Just like a grownup, and how to spell
Chrysanthemum.

At night I lay in a small white room
On a narrow cot strung with cords
And slept and dreamed my childhood dreams
While the bantam chicks poked for worms
In the weeds outside.

They tell me that Parachinar,
My childhood home,
Is home to Al-Qaeda now,
A Madrassah training camp.

Who sleeps now in the small white room,
On the narrow cot strung with cords,
And do dreams still float in space
While the bantam chicks poke for worms
In the weeds outside?

Erica Massender

SHADOW GIRL

If you go on Second Street you'll find a girl who lives in the shadows, this girl has been in the dark so long her hair is as black as night, her skin as pasty, pale as a blank piece of unlined paper and her eyes are as icy cold as the Arctic Ocean from the top of the world. But this girl's story doesn't end in bitterness and despair because if you go down the road, cross the street and take a left you'll find a boy with hair like rough wheat fields, his skin as tan as the Hawaiian beach, eyes sweet as golden glistening honey and a smile so bright and so warm it could replace the sun.

Most importantly this boy can lead Shadow Girl out of the darkness and into the light...

He just has to find her first.

Kim Nuzzo

WONDERFUL DISASTER

The holy man
alone in the ruin
wearing a party dress
laughing.

Suddenly
he is happy
in the lost paradise
of childhood.

Between vultures and bones
he finds white petals and
a thousand beautiful mistakes.

Valerie Haugen

FAMILY VISITATION

Three nights in a row
I dream of my dead.
My mother, dying again,
is lying in my daughter's bed.
My dream self rises
and goes to her.
Another voice, mine,
says this is a dream
and she is not real.
She is dead. I feel her arm
to prove this to myself.
She feels as real as I do.
She speaks to me.
I won't listen.
I tell her she is dead.
You are dead, you are dead,
you cannot speak to me,
you are dead.
Another night, I dream
of my dead baby. In this dream,
she has been murdered, I find her
in a plastic bag. I rage,
I grieve. This dream
traps me
again and again and again.
My dead father visits
my dreams. Please, I say,
you are dead, don't visit me.
He says, so clearly, in his voice,
which must only be my imagination,
because he is dead,

he is dead,
he says he only came
to tell me
I should listen
to my mother.

Will they live forever
in my dreams?
Do they come
so that I can remind them
they are dead?
Do they come to tell me to live
before I die?

David Romtvedt

FOOTBALL FIELD, BUTARE, RWANDA, 1977

1.

The white man ascends the platform
with the foreign friends of the nation,
another umuzungu in line to meet
President Habyarimana Juvenal.
Though he's been told not to,
he looks into the President's eyes,
the flecks of gold swimming
in the whites. Juvenal gazes
to the other end of the field
where the Intore Dancers hammer
the ground with their bare feet,
the dusty jingling rising from bells
tied to their ankles and calves.
Still not looking at him, Juvenal
takes the *umuzungu*'s hand, holds it
a little too tightly, a little too long,
says, *"Les amis du pays."*

2.

The white man plays softball
with the *Québécois coopérants
étrangers,* shirts and hats for bases.
A long fly to center and he backs up
across the field to the bleachers
built by German colonialists
before the world gave Rwanda
to the Belgians. He clambers up
three rows, arms outstretched.
The ball falls into his glove

like the first flake of snow falling
onto his tongue when he was a child.
The players whistle and cheer
and the shortstop runs to him,
thumps him on the back and shouts,
"Mais ça, ça c'est bon, ça."
A really good catch.

3.

The white man falls in love
with a local woman. They walk
to a cinder block bar with a tin roof
and drink Primus in liter bottles.
The barman's twelve-year-old daughter
plays the same six *soukous* records
over and over, the polyrhythmic songs
spinning the dancers into two worlds.
The woman touches the man's waist,
says, *"Tu vois, non?"* Hip like this,
shoulder here. The floor is littered
with peanut shells and happiness,
and the laughter in the room is as warm
as the night. When the moon goes down,
the man and woman walk to the field.
In the open expanse where no one sees,
they lie in the dust and make love
as if history never happened.

First published in The Same Magazine.

Lynda La Rocca

CHARTING THIS COURSE

My life is my message. —Mahatma Gandhi

I am a maker of lists.
Words scrawled on scraps of paper
remind me that
I must buy eggs
and fresh cream cheese,
bake pumpkin bread,
call Alice,
write that article,
rake leaves.
Numbered tasks to make me useful,
create order,
forge a meaning
while I'm bobbing on
some salty sea,
my feet touching no bottom.
Listing, I am listing,
writing reasons
for my being.
Come tomorrow, early morning,
back on earth,
I'm picking purple grapes
and planting orange poppies.
But tonight I pencil in a slot
for dancing underneath
white stars
to music
I'm composing
as I go.

Previously published in The Stillness Between *by Lynda La Rocca (2009, Pudding House Publications, Ohio)*

Roger Adams

GYPSIES AT THE POOL

There is a photo I saw
of a minivan sitting on
the bottom of a swimming pool.
The driver is telling a cop,
"I got confused."

He is on a chair
sees himself by the pool
paying the sawbuck he thought
was protected.   Duty fulfilled
the legacy stays mapped, safe.

The kid knows but doesn't see.
That image is years off,
when witnesses are dead,
when enemies writing obituaries gone too.
He closes his eyes, relaxes.

Gypsies are at the pool now
cooking meat on a fire,
making a punchbowl,
dancing,
tuning violins.

The music is before its time.
The money is gone.
The Roma can't swim.
The van won't start.
The cop is writing a ticket.

Marjorie DeLuca

VEGETARIAN DOGS

We are lying around,
me by the stove
Bear by the worn and rickety door,
where there are plenty of good fall smells.

Dinner had been the usual:
kibbles, veggies, rice.
She's a good cook,
but usually the same stuff.

Bear gets up, circles, tail shifting,
looks at me, flops back down.
I roll over and look back at him.
I send a brain message, What?

He sends back, Something
happening outside. Smells
really good, but I don't know the scent.
I send back to Bear, Let's take a look.

Bear's a bit younger
so I let him take over.
He starts to make new
squeaking noises in his throat.

They think we have to pee.
They hate pee inside.
She jumps up and gets
the leashes, snaps them on us.

When she pulls open the door
the scent on the air is crazy, makes me dizzy.
Bear isn't pretending now.
Hits the screen door hard with a paw.

The smell makes me tremble.
She takes her time on the stoop
putting on knit gloves.
We figured she smells it too,
but seems not to notice.

Bear moves first, confidently
snaps the leash and
jumps off the stoop. Runs.
I go next, right on his tail.

Across the street at the Murphy's,
Jerry is taking stuff out of his
pickup. It all smells like the woods.
He has something dead
with a freshly slit throat,

head hanging out the back,
tongue lifeless out the side of
its mouth, stream of red stuff
pouring into the gutter.

Bear sends a thought: It's getting away,
drops down on his belly in the gutter,
lapping up the red stuff. He's right.
Such a heady scene. I drop down too.

Lapping…lapping. She screams.
Leashes, snapped, dangle from our collars.
Jerry's arms drop, hands over mouth,
can't speak. We lap…lap…snort…gag.

She grabs Bear by his collar
yanks him up to sitting,
red stuff dripping from his belly.
She drags me up too and ties us together
with the rest of the leash.

Jerry stifles a laugh behind his hand.

She drags us back to our stoop,
smearing the sidewalks red with wet fur,
slurping around our snouts to savor each drop.

She yanks us together around the side to the
back yard, fastening the gate loudly,
and hoses us down with cold water.
We sleep outside in the cold that night.

No one would talk about it in the morning.

José Alcantara

TWO DEGREES

He throws a grappling hook at the sky
catches on the red rim of Mars
and begins to climb.
But the mind slips
too weak to carry the weight.
He tumbles back to hard road
a dog on a leash
his son waiting for breakfast.
He stumbles back toward the house.
The sun creeps closer to the ridge.
Mars tucks its head beneath a light blue blanket.

Art Goodtimes

ORVIS HOT SPRINGS

Even on the Norwood
side of Dallas Divide
it's starting to be

that kind of San Juan cold
that rousts us from our snug acre
looking south to Lone Cone

Snow you can actually hear
rapping like a raven
against the glass

Siberian elms' low
groans between gusts
& the knee deep cold

Just then's when we bundle up
Put her into overdrive
& head down Norwood Hill

Swerving for every
"Rock in the road!" "Rock in the road!"
Curving through the San Miguel Cañon

Up Leopard Creek & then down
to the Uncompahgre. Fifty miles
to the hot springs

Just to see
steam billowing
Orion rising

And once again
to be buck naked
in the Rockies' wild embrace

First published in the Telluride Watch *and the* Four Corners Free Press *(Cortez).*

Catherine Garland

DIRGE FOR 75,000
ELEPHANTS

I have watched the pregnancy, the getting bigger month by month,
The matriarch of the elephant herd, looked up to for wisdom and
    guidance.
In this tender time of begetting, the others in the herd, sisters, aunts,
Nieces, daughters, protect her, do their best to shield her, shade her,
Deeply cherish her.

In China, a young man, Buddhist, holds out a carving, an ivory carving,
Intricately worked, exquisite craftsmanship. I admire the beauty, then ask,
What of the elephant from whom this ivory came? He smiles.
    That elephant
Gifted me her tusks and that elephant now is blessed. It is a good thing,
A very good thing that I have given honor to this elephant with this carving
Of much beauty. And he smiles again. A happy Buddhist smile.

A newspaper clipping tells of Chinese diplomats flying their private planes
Into elephant territory. They have diplomatic immunity, and with impunity
Load large piles of elephant tusks inside. These will be sold at great profit
To the dealers, who will sell at even greater profit to the artists,
    who will sell
At even greater profit to the tourists.

I drive out in my Jeep to the spot where I last saw the pregnant female,
Matriarch of her tribe. Her time is due, her time of joy, and I want
    to be there,
Celebrate for her. As I draw close, I see a cloud ahead, a cloud of buzzing
Insects. And then the stench enfolds me in the open jeep. In the clearing
The elephant lies on her side. Her face is eviscerated, her tusks hacked off
And gone. A swarm of yellow maggots shrouds her, painting the huge
Hulk a dull gold in the morning light. Her infant, aborted in the slaughter,

Lies dying in a pool of blood.

Her tusks are on their way to China now. They will make
    many people rich and
Happy—the diplomats, the dealers, the artists, the tourists.
    And my friend,
Matriarch of her herd, lies rotting in her stench, her long-awaited baby
At her side.

Sandra Dorr

PERIGEE

If you could see the moon tonight—
if you could see the moon, Mother.

The crust has fallen away,
its white shell pure as sound, a wave
still rolling through the night.

How can I reach you? Or put my arms
around your shoulders
and ask you to tell me a story again.

The whole orb: how it glitters.
Such a simple thing yet nothing
on this earth can make it happen.

No more than I can see you, my dear.
Did I ever feel such love, such perfect light
when we were together, and the dark shadow

always near? Did I ever see you
in such radiance as that which holds our planet
right now? Right now

if I could touch the soft sprayed curls
on your head, and hear you laugh on the phone
as you did, even in the bitter pain

you were like a girl—so pleased to get the call,
to be teased—ah, such spirit. To see you again,
to hear you laugh, I would walk inch by inch,

mile by mile up through the stars
until my feet were on the round, full moon.

First published in the Manzanita Quarterly. *Subsequently published in* Desert Water (*Lithic Press,* 2009).

Charles Braddy

THOSE CROWS

This morning the crows woke me up.
I was trying to sleep.
They didn't care.
Two crows,
fighting over marshmallows.
Two crows,
blindly breaking paradise.

Catherine Garland

THE COLOR OF LOVE

When we make love, I ask,
what color is it? Is it Red
for passion, the red of a sun
setting the sky on fire? A ripe
plum, ready to spill its juices?
Or is it Green? A green of
ecstasy and bliss, a folding
into each other, a sacred
Oneness. Or maybe Blue,
the color of eternity, love
stretching into the beyond
forever. Or is it White, a
blinding light obliterating all
else, complete unto itself?
Maybe a shy Pink, virginal
almost, a coming together
of two neophytes. Or Yellow?
Surely it must be yellow. A golden
yellow, shining light on What Is,
What Was and What will be to come.

Ed Cross

ASPEN DAY

Grey sky, no wind, brisk and clear
Eight new inches; no need for fear
The snow, deep and soft,
Waiting; a virgin bride
The quiet calm of the chairlift ride
The day begins.
And now, down the mountain, turning
The snow, billowing, churning
Chest high, in the quiet of the trees
The only sound
The carving of your skis
Left and right, and always down
Diving, driving
Seeking, experiencing
The closeness of nature
Such is why
I ski to live
and live to ski.

Sandra Dexter

TWILIGHT

Delicate, brittle bones
Being set aside
  Piece by piece
Ever so gently
Why didn't I keep them
  Intact?

Old, brittle memories
Die away
Disintegrate

A new day
  Dawns
A pale orange
Not as bright as
  Expected

Danny Rosen

ALL OUR FATHERS

Wasn't our fault all the homes were closed, locked and barred,
or that the churches went door to door,
or that the revelers had such sad eyes—
their message of peace the smallest font,
or that wanting out of the war zone was all the pilgrim's sought.
Wasn't our fault the onslaught of returned gifts began
with diamonds no longer holding the heart, but the gun,
and everyone sunk to having fun, on the very day the graves were found.
Wasn't our fault the youngest son bought the farm so young.
He clutched, fell back, dropped like a stone, over and over again he died
so real, better than the TV dead, shot in the back on the front yard hill.
What tough children we were, living with the bullseye on the town square,
where the railroad screamed and the donkey said, all our fathers
were hunters kid.

Suzanne Bronson

THAT GLASS SLIPPER

Cinderella's sister was just a lonely thing.
A deliberate, willing thing.
She cut off her toes to make the shoe fit
and I've held that hatchet myself.

Roger Adams

POETA EN SUEÑO

Por un rato
solamente,
unos minutos
namas,
vuelo con ella.

Entre dos vidas
separadas en
tiempo
pero unidos en viaje.
Seguimos carreteras lejanos
por carriles
juntos.

Espíritus y almas
colgados a un tapiz
pintado de sangre,
lagrimas y deseos.

La escultura que fabrican
amanece conjunto
de brazos, muñecas y dedos.
Pensando en ambos
palabras de un solo
corazón.

Veo colores brillantes;
espliego,
carmesí,
verde. Tinto entre
las plumas detrás
ojos
cerrados.

Marilyn McDonald

A POEM

A poem is like sea foam
That washes on the sand:
Giving, taking, and sharing
with the land.

A poem is like a flame
That casts a gentle glow
Upon the thoughts of life, and love,
and other things we know.

A poem is an eternal force
That lives when all else dies;
To hold the breath of life,
and gently cast a sigh.

Don McIver

AN APOLOGY TO AND FOR
MY ANCESTORS

for Charles Lloyd

A title, deed, certificate of ownership,
has my grandmother's maiden name.
There's a history, a geography of roots
that almost makes it so.
Missouri, a slave state,
compromised into existence
and that's where we landed before the Civil War.

How do you honor your ancestors
    and not apologize for their mistakes?

There's an open space with my name on it,
a space that once belonged to all,
to the people,
to the earth itself.
Montana, Texas, Colorado,
we're just living where we land
and landed with a thud.

Lawton Eddy

HOME IS WHERE
THE HEART IS

Delta jet lets me loose in San Francisco where you greet me
with too many questions, and I seek sushi impatiently

"You've lived for more than five years in a town without sushi?"
you say
"A town spelled Saleeda, called Salida, where you can't even go out
dancing on a regular basis?"

Your eyes are full of disbelief
your hair full of wind

Thank you friend, for your concern
But let's sit, I say, and share a spider roll
and I'll tell you about the heart on the mountain
and the guys in the hardware store who know my name

the jeweler who cleans my rings for the price of a smile
and the man in the tire shop who scolds me like a dad
when my tread is worn too thin

And here, in this river town, I have a teacher
who played the violin with the Metropolitan Opera
sometimes he says "excellent" when I hit the notes—just right

Do you know there's a stage in the old steam plant
where townfolk from 5 to 75 come to sing, tap dance
and tell their stories bravely
for an audience that always claps their hands

And let me tell you 'bout the wimmin in this town

who believe elections are important
Who spent more hours on the phone and knocking on doors
than most of us spend complaining about the state of this world
and that's a lot

So I take trips to the city for sushi, and dance when I can
in circles of wimmin who move like their hips'll give birth to tomorrow
But mostly I'm just home

So thank you friend, for you do know me well
but please, don't ask how I can do without this happening thing
or that kind of action
Ask how my town embraces me, and if my people are here
'cuz that is what you really want to know

Your chopsticks stir wasabi into a soy sauce paste
you flash a sideways smile at me and say
Tell me more about the heart on the mountain…

Previously published in the chapbook, On Stage: River City Nomads, Poetry Performances Volume One
2004–2009

David Romtvedt

DANCING IN ZAÏRE

Hot afternoons we swam across the lake
and walked home along the shore, stopping
in town at the music shop. On the counter
ten portable turntables were going at once.
When somebody left, you jumped forward
and asked for Lipua Lipua or Dr. Nico
or l'Orchestre African Fiesta and the man
who ran the shop took the 45RPM record
from its sleeve, touching only the edges,
and handed it to you, and by the time
somebody finally bought a record,
it'd have a million scratches.

Near sunset, we walked to the market
where the old women sat on mats selling
paper pyramids of roasted groundnuts
and ten kilo bags of rice filled with rocks.
The old men drank in the still hot shade
of the pavilion's corrugated metal roof—
banana and sorghum beer sucked through
long straws from fifty-five gallon drums.
We stood and talked about *l'authenticité*.

It felt good and we forgot we were speaking
French and not Kiswahili, Lingala, or Tshiluba.
President Mobutu outlawed ties and jackets
as signs of European bondage, and renamed
our country Zaïre and the river Zaïre and even
the money Zaïre. No one was called *madame*
or *monsieur*. We were *citoyen* and *citoyenne*.
It was beautiful to be equal.

We picked new names. Joseph-Désiré Mobutu
became Mobutu Sese Seko Nkuka Ngbendu
wa Za Banga—the all-powerful warrior who
because of his endurance and indefatigable
will to win goes from conquest to conquest
leaving fire in his wake. It was exciting
to think we might be free.

Maybe it's not fair to say it ended up as bad
as before. We went to Mobutu's compound
and, hiding from the soldiers, climbed the fence.
We could see the flowers and trees, the fruit
fallen to the ground, uneaten. They said
Mobutu had elephants but I don't know.

Where we lived there were only monkeys
screeching in the trees. It wasn't so hot
and it was too high for tsetse flies
so no sleeping sickness though we had malaria.
All through the rainy season, we made fires
to drive away the mosquitoes. I loved the smoke
and mist, the sweet smell of burning garbage
and eucalyptus leaves, and dancing at night
in leaking pavilions to the scratched records
someone had bought in the shop.

Barbara Ford

POP KOANS

1.

In the yoga studio a tick
crawls onto your leg.
As you head to the bathroom
to flush it, one of your students
asks, "didn't you take a vow
of nonviolence?" Carrying the tick
outside, you notice how good you feel.

      a. apply first thought, best thought to the above scenario.
      b. who is nobler: the tick, the student, or you?
      c. was the room's vibration raised by your action?
      d. what would Buddha do?

2.

Your cat plays with a chipmunk
in the manner of a squeezy toy.
Horrified, you phone your friend
who advises you to stop looking.

      a. apply lovingkindness to this situation.
      b. discuss 'right livelihood' for chipmunks.
      c. is it beneficial to have all your friends on speed dial?
      d. can cats take a vow of non-violence?

3.

Your friend on the phone wishes the now dead chipmunk
a swift rebirth into a more cat-proof life form, suggesting
it could return as a tick on the lawn of your yoga student.

a. do you need different friends?
b. if this were a dream, what would Sigmund and Carl
   disagree about?
c. outline the Zen of predation.
d. write a haiku about your experience, bonus points for obfuscation.

Previously published in Spillway #20, Summer 2013

Heidi Owen

CORVIDAE

In a world where magic has gone skittish,
Raven remains a shape-shifter,
first huge as a cow on this desert highway,
then, in off-kilter hops, small as a sparrow
in the ditch.

These Southern ravens are sleek.
They imitate crows, pretend to be polite,
but black against the colors of the world,
caught plotting strategy,
or beak-deep in deer carcass, tugging, ripping,
any shim of illusion vanishes.

Far North in an island rainforest
where winters are heavy and dark,
ravens barter among the houses.
Feathers bristle up behind their beaks.
They strut.
Overstuffed garbage cans send them suddenly busy.
Diapers, junk-food wrappers, human vices
scattered on the road.

The whistle of black wings overhead,
the sound of stones dropped in a pool,
the harsh call.

One winter, snow fell early.
By February, even eagles set down in town to scavenge.
The tricksters had no tricks, the shape-shifters
were starving.

Our education said let the wildlife stay wild—
free food kills freedom.
One day outside the backdoor, three ravens
stared at us with flat eyes,
then turned away to peck at dog shit
by the road.
We took the frost-burned meat
from the corners of the freezer,
laid it out in the snow.

But here and now, these Southern birds
are full of themselves,
full on roadside fine dining,
shifting larger and smaller in the hot sun.

Marjorie DeLuca

INSOMNIA

Monsters
party under
my bed

To-do list
does a jig
in my head

Night tiptoes
by on
little cat pads

nails clicking
like the ticking
of the clock

Lynda La Rocca

HOUSEGUEST FROM HELL
(or, Hello, you must be going)

I've locked the keys inside the car,
but that won't mar
my day because
(Applause! Applause!)
I have another set right here.
So never fear,
we'll make your flight.
It may be tight,
but you'll be on that plane today
and on your way—
out of my sight,
to my delight.

Ron Byers

THE IMPORTANCE OF
GIBBERISH

Gibberish…the unexpected juxtaposition of words…gateway to the surreal
…the axle grease that lubricates little used parts of the mind
…a tease for left brained primates on their way to extinction

Gibberish…is like a poem hidden in wet cement
you only know it's there from the gas bubbles
        …it's where you realize…you really can't explain
        …anything after all…you really should retire from
        reasons

Gibberish…is a safety valve for psychotic behavior
It helps us safely exchange bodily fluids
While wearing our rubber diapers of convention
…it's when you're throat talk croaking like a frog
on a Lilly pad

Gibberish…is like a kiss from a big lipped dancing hippo
Doing the Dervish twirl in your darkened bedroom
…it's what you say after the priest fondles you
on the way to the gallows
…it's like a Rorschach test for netting God
after the oxygen runs out in your shrink-wrap world

Gibberish…is where ya do what ya gotta do while ya
pray for an intervention
…it's like a yard show where you don't care what the
neighbors think
…it's what would happen if you lived with your
parents until the age of 40

Gibberish…is the windmill of succulent afterthoughts
caught by surprise in the night light…
on the way to where waves & particles are the same
…it's the mysterious fluttering under the leaf pile

Gibberish…is the juice from a thousand squeezed stories
stains on the tablecloth…
food stuck between your teeth
…it's some lame explanation for premature death
a sweet cake filling squished on the highway

Gibberish…is like a conversation with an intruder who duck tapes your mouth
and
demands to know the combination
…it's like giving directions to a lesser God…while gargling
with holy hallelujah mouth wash
…it's what ya say at a baptismal bath when someone pulls the drain plug
on your way to ecstasy

Gibberish…is an improvisational tool ta get ya out of trouble
…it's like talking underwater…tryin to tell them you want out of this dunk tank
…it's when words are no match for the deed you have witnessed
so you babble as they take you away

Gibberish…is what ya sound like when you're all
rolled up inside a luminescent burrito
…is what ya say when ya find out there were cliff notes
for enlightenment…& ya wasted all this time
…is what ya say when you get a hole-in-one…
but it wasn't at the golf course

Gibberish…is what ya say to the judge for giving
You a long sentence…for reading between the lines
…is what a falling trapeze artist says right before landing in the elephant poop
…is what ya start saying when you keep calling out
& calling out…& nobody ever gets back to you

Gibberish…is like love…ya don't know what it is when it's
dissected and floppin on the table
…it's like an old tune ya heard in the distance…
on a day when the smoke came over the mountains

Gibberish…is like a bad idea that came into its own sweet merciful resuscitation
…and is now…a good idea

Gibberish…is all the things you wish you had said in this short, contorted dream

David Teitler

TEMPLE OF LITERATURE

I am a father now
and a time traveler

I am banyan tree
smiling at scholars tossing their caps

I am stone lion
marveling at smartly dressed teens posing by my side

I am Confucius
gilded in gold, blessing those at my feet

Yesterday, I was pregnant with expectations
embarking on a road to unknown places

Tomorrow, I travel back in time
to a daughter lost to dragons and mist

Perhaps I am not so much a time traveler
as a man walking a circular path

Each pass a bit grayer, a bit more baggage
a bit more secure as I pass familiar landmarks

Rosemerry Wahtola Trommer
LONG NIGHT IN ABIQUIU

All night, they wrestled
inside me, the angel
who pulls you in closer
and the angel who shoves
you away. They tussled
and grappled and pushed back
my stomach, my spleen, my gallbladder
to make enough space
for the brawl. What could
I do but lay there, moaning,
not even recalling which one
I was rooting for, just longing
for them to stop. In the morning,
they were both exhausted,
having rearranged each other's
ribs. Each conceded the other
had a compelling case and
went out for coffee, leaning
on each other's shoulders
as they left, leaving me
with an emptiness so great
a whole flock of ravens
flew through.

Cathleen Treacy

ANOTHER WAKING DREAM

I am quite amazed
At the things that
We do
With the places we've
Been
Strung out like
Scarecrows
Across our horizons.

Give credence to
Wrongs
And balance to
Rights
Made money
Out of memories
And fought
Wars with the tiniest
Of beliefs.

Based philosophies
On images
Carved out of someone
else's destiny
Mined religions
On someone else's
Death.

Found love in
Ruins of another's
World
And spent moments

Too long
Seeking our own
Forever
In rocks
Strewn across fields.

Logan Cross

THE RIVER WE PADDLE:
A METAPHOR ABOUT LIFE

The simple tranquility of the river
It is a serenity that lives in the middle of nowhere
Many do not know it exists
Many never get to experience it
Many have no idea they are missing it
Every river is different
Although the idea seems the same
The journey is what matters
Each moves in a creative pattern
Allowing space for each maneuver & obstacle
The true beauty of the river
Lies deep within the shallows
And thick around the bends
Not knowing exactly what waits around the next corner
But it is the river and whatever terrain it is
You are ready
If you take advantage of it
Power on in full force
Constantly curving, dipping and spinning
A wild movement that carries you through
Not without help
Strong through the rapids
Clever with your path
The river waits for no one
Make no mistake
It will punish you for your errors
And reward you for your defeats
The water might splash you
The current could flip you
The rocks will easily stray you

But the sun does come out
And nothing is more appreciated than the warmth of the sun
Upon a shivering river rat
The forgiveness of the river is soothing
A natural therapy
Peacefulness of the mind
Drifting and joking down the calm water
Sweet wine drizzling into your mouth
The comfort of being on land after a long day
The refreshed embody of being in the bare outdoors
Feeling complete after a family meal
The joy of a perfectly made S'more
Singing songs and telling stories around the fire
Falling asleep beneath a blanket of stars
You wake up with sand between your toes
Your clothes still damp with yesterday's adventures
But you climb back aboard that boat
And you paddle on
Because nothing is as gorgeous
As the travels of the river.

Marjorie DeLuca

MOM'S NAP

She wasn't a cuddler
nor a kisser
not even a hugger
but she was my Mom.

Never did she sleep next to me,
cuddling me in the dark.
Never did I get much more
than a BandAid on a booboo.

> *She treated us like aliens.*
> *But I knew all that.*

Then her soul departed,
leaving her body for us
to care for like an old dress
no one would ever wear again.

She wasn't sure who I was
but wanted me to know the
big picture on the dresser is
her boyfriend Jimmy. He is a good kisser.

> *But I knew him as Daddy.*
> *Pictures of the aliens were nearby.*

In her little room now, the afternoon
slows as the elder care wing grows quiet
and she lies down on her twin bed
under the covers for her daily nap.

Do you want to lie with me? she asks.
I lie down beside her on top of the covers
and drape my arm across her waist.
At last she falls asleep in my grasp.

Sandra Dorr

MIRAGE

Years of shouting, slamming doors,
breaking the small dishes,
leaving the room in mid-air

vanish into the ringing mountain,
steeple-topped cupolas, a walk
on stone streets of fresh snow, dinner
in a bistro.   White lights shine,
iced pearls on tiny streets.

This surprising tenderness when
you cup my hand in your pocket
and ask, Are you cold?
What do you want to do?
We hurry through the town.

Are you all right?
Yes. Yes. I am.
We're three blocks from our hotel
in air so frigid our shoes crack
the black ice of the street.

Look. A buck and a doe,
skinny from the mountain,
nuzzle trees in a snowy yard.
They step out, prancing, framed
under the streetlight in a painting.

A new stillness fills us.
Nothing wanting, nothing to want.
Everything we have given has come back.

First published in a chapbook, Desert Water *(Lithic Press, 2009).*

Micah Franz
ATOMIC

Disestablishmentarianism,
Never a wrong time to rhyme.
Divide this schism.
Into what is;
and what isn't-isms.

We're all human,
crew-men,
In the lumen of life.

Like Harry Truman
I drop bombs.
On a metaphorical rampage
To reveal the truth.

Barbara Ford

BLUEPRINT

House with Vault of Skull
Window of Eye, Floor of Bone

oh my hammer, my chisel, my whistle, my shadow

Refuge with Fountain of Blood
Wall of Skin, Current of Breath

oh my clockworks, my sump pump, my pup tent, my echo

Shelter with Ridge of Spine
Door of Mouth, Ceiling of Sinew

oh my mule, my chassis, my paradox, my yes and no

Armature with Beams of Tendons
Terrain of Muscle, Parade of Cells

oh my library, my camel, my coffin, my minstrel show

Periscope, Colony, Metaphor of More and Less
Galaxy of Geography
Altar of Biology

oh my vessel, my crucible, my chalice

infinite friend, true blue foe

Karen Day

WEST-TEXAS
HALLOWEEN BLUES, 1946

Saturday, first thing after Halloween,
mother
drops us both in a galvanized tub &
hoses us down
out by the clothesline.

Just the two of us:
Leonard and me,
in child love already,
and now
buck-naked in
a tub of West-Texas precious water.

My mother scrubs away
crepe paper stains and glitter and chocolate,
and the ever-present oily dust stuck
between our toes.

Across the alley
Leonard's house,
identical to ours,
white, with a small back porch,
rests on blocks.

His mother, Ruby,
sits at her upright piano
and wails to God:
"So I'll cherish the old rugged cross...!"

Mother warns me
I should be reverent
and hum along,

but
my eyes are *stuck* on
that "thing" between Leonard's legs.

I check myself. Where? Where is mine?
Maybe next year when I turn six?

Now a grown man, big and grizzled,
Leonard trucks oil
from rusty storage tanks
to the refinery at Odessa.

Our old clapboard houses—
dozens of them—were moved
over to that rig at Pecos.

Mother and Ruby have
gone to live in God's house.

And myself?
When Halloween rolls around each year,
I think about this:

Come back,
clothesline.

Come back,
washtub.

Come back,
Leonard
and Ruby
and mother.

Come back,
old rugged cross.

Previously published in Sugar Mule, *issue 37.*

Stewart S. Warren

SELF EMPLOYED

For a long time I was on my way
to get a real job. But the sun
kept coming up in different places
and each evening it left
whistling a new song.
I felt compelled to record all this
so I followed the shifting light,
the way it ran looping colored circles
around the world, then disappeared
behind tides of prairie and dark mountains.

> *Oh, that's just the sun, they said,*
> *let's go make some hay.*

One day I followed the sun
into the night, and found all
its companions in a great migration
as far as I could see;
and someone was standing
there, awestruck, looking,
but I could no longer say his name,
and there was no longer
any job but this
to which I could return.

Sarah Pletts

A POET IS?

On a German plane over the North Sea

You think a poet is?
A poet lives to
Get up and write
About something that cooked her.
A poet dances on the sun
And comes home to swim.
A poet eats surrounded by people laughing.
A poet is courage
To know thyself.
And tell you.
Not for profit
or gain.
Or even love.
But to be or not to be.
You know where you are with a poet.

Rett Harper

THE HAIR CUT

When I walked into your hospital room,
I hardly recognized you with your cheeks sunken.
You were all eyes and teeth and long white hair,
no longer my giant father—so old for sixty-nine.
"Your mother tells me you cut hair," you said.
"Oh just my husband's and my son's hair," I hedged.
Then your, "I'd appreciate it if you'd cut mine,"
put me on the spot. No one but a professional
had ever cut that fine, thin curly hair.
Even mother who was always cutting and styling
kids', friends' and her own hair wouldn't
touch it. Touch it? I couldn't remember ever…
Yet I couldn't refuse this rare direct request
because we all knew you were dying.

The next morning you called early wanting
to "get this show on the road."
Your impatience to be doing something
left no room for my jet lag.
I bought new scissors on the way
because mother did not want
her old ones to be blamed.
Fearing a big blunt mistake, it seemed
I cut each unforgiving hair separately,
enjoying the time and the touch
and easy small talk until
you said, "You'd never make a living at this.
You take too long."
Earnestly, as I had always done,
I tried to defend myself:
"I'm not trying to make a living at this.

I cut only the hair of those I love."
Then I flashed, "What's the matter old man,
you got someplace else to go?"
You smiled at that.
You always liked it
when I could be tough.

The next time I saw you,
you were not there.
Our family stood around your coffin
And my small son said it for us all,
"I want to touch him."
So we each did. At my turn
I stroked your hair.
"Nice hair cut. Thanks Dad."

Valerie Haugen
A MOTHER'S LOVE

Speaking to the young man
who says he loves my daughter,
I let the words come gently
(and I hear my grandmother's
southern drawl
on the far coast of my voice),
warmly, with tenderness,
kindness, with my open heart.
I speak to this young man,
and say as simply as I can,
the better he should understand,
"If you hurt my daughter,
or harm comes to her
on your watch, in any way—
I will kill you...
in the ancient way...
meaning with a tire iron.

Ron Byers

THE SAUCE BOSS

The sauce boss tell me he gonna make it taste good
even if I don't like what I'm eating.
My past was like a sore & swollen sea urchin
washed up on a prickly shore.
So he throw my miserable self into the gumbo pot
& start singing a happy tune
He simmer my fat-brain sorrow pie into a tub of lard laughter
And baste my misery monologue with a see-thru sauce
Like I never taste before
Then he serve me up as my future-self soup of the day.

Sandra Dorr

WALKING WITH JULIAN

Out of the school box,
my son and I drop down
the canyon cleft
into shining ricegrass
where deer last night slept.
We step into the quiet
held by the rigid tips

of magenta prickly pear
scattered through the basin,
their seeds hard
inside their sepulchered fruit.
Invisible sounds
fall from the cactus root
to this soft crust of ground.

I edge through still-flowering mallow
with he who grew within me
like the hundreds of gold stems
around us, swaying
in the waning light, far and away
into which we will blossom.
Spreading his long fingers,

Julian leaves space
for my shadow, brushing
the pink four-winged saltbrush
with his still-young skin,
his dark eyes taking
the desert in.
Above us three dun deer

spring off ledges.
Ghost horses drift off cliffs,
become petroglyphs,
over and on we travel the ravine
of an old flowing stream.
Autumn boy, brown-gold hair
thick as water, walking on air.

He knows the touch
of this land, how time floats
under white clouds.
High up, ravens circle fallen boulders.
Inside, the rock turns black,
smells cool and weedy, dark,
androgynous.   Welling up

from the egg of the earth,
hidden sweet water.
We rub our hands over rough
volcanic rock, set in a circle
where people once drew together.
We feel the presence of what was,
as if all summer, this wind

rattling the cottonwoods,
blowing over the meadow,
was gathered in this quiet bowl.
My son so tall he must bend down
to hug me. It's all I can do
to stand upright.
My face against his heart.

First published in a chapbook, Desert Water (*Lithic Press, 2009*).

Kathleen Maris

ALMOST MAY

In your mother's
Santa Rita bed

You are perfectly still
Let the migratory

White-winged dove approach
Black ants do not crawl

I saguaro stand
With 31 arms drip morphine

Enough to kill the pain
Not enough to kill the man

I ocotillo sway
Grow crimson flowers

During this rain
You are still dying

Richard Newman

LITTLE FUGUE OF
LOVE AND DEATH

We talked of the end of the world and then
We sang us a song, and then sang it again.
— Woody Guthrie, "This Dusty Old Dust"

The sky is gray. My joints are old.
The terrorists will nuke us.
I cannot shake this summer cold.
My head's a hive of mucous.

Our dog is old. He cannot shake.
He collapses in the iris.
Dead birds litter the alleyway,
a wave of West Nile virus.

We drink beneath the new flight path
the clouds can't hope to deaden.
We can't see T-birds, Raptors, Blackhawks,
but it sounds like Armageddon.

And you and I sit on our porch,
drenched head to toe in Deet.
We swill the High Life, holding hands
despite the record heat.

The dog has grayed. The sky has grayed.
The grass and shrubs have browned.
Our life is high. The sky is low.
Our love goes round and round.

From Domestic Fugues *(Steel Toe Books, 2009). Originally appeared in* Boulevard *(Volume 24, 2008)*
and also on Verse Daily, 2009

David Feela

"POEMS THAT TOUCH YOU"
(title in a bookstore)

I've read poetry that didn't
touch me, and the truth is—
if I had to choose—I'd prefer
what's less invasive.
Sadness, rage, hormonal
indiscretion—it all amounts to
a form of lyrical masturbation
like a Shakespearean sonnet
that couples with itself
in the last two lines.
I do not want any indiscriminate
touching when I pick a book
off the shelf and stand in the aisle
reading a page or two,
clueless as to what I'll feel.
Boundaries assert themselves
in a world so random.
Once I touched a girl
who didn't expect it,
a sweet spot she preferred
to keep to herself.
To her, I am no different
than the poem she had
to memorize in the fifth grade
and has since forgotten.
If art imitates life
then let us not be touched
when all we want
is to be moved.

Lynda La Rocca

TRESPASS

He was here,
eyes reflected in the
midnight kitchen window.
But those are my eyes,
his eyes
that he gave to me,
that blinked
and I was born.
On a peg in the
hallway for 20 years,
I hang his sweater,
heavy with dust.
The photographs I burned,
but I still see him,
I can smell him.
And the moaning, when I hear it
now just means
that
upstairs
somebody is dreaming,
maybe someone's cold.

Originally published in Spiral *by Lynda La Rocca (2012, Liquid Light Press, Colorado)*

Valerie Haugen

FUCKING AND FIGHTING

Here in the Valhalla Apartments
(if you lived here, you'd be home now)
the apartments on either side
of the poet who lives alone
are inhabited by couples.
One couple makes love at night,
the other early in the morning.
The walls are made of yesterday's
newspaper. The windows are made
of yesterday's sky.
On one side, they love like wounded doves,
on the other, like a lion making a kill,
the hyenas circle laughing, hungry.
Five minutes later the lion
roars at his mate to shut
the fuck up. The afterglow
is light by which
to write a poem.

David Feela

PASTURES OF EDEN

Before I understood how hunger
makes a creature mean, my uncle pointed
to the cows on the other side of his fence.

I asked if I could pet one; he said no,
that farm animals were not for pleasure.
I asked if cows drank milk. Once again, no.

Then he plucked a long stem of grass,
stuck it in the space between his front teeth.
I picked one too, gnawed it like a green fuse.

It must have been my first rumination,
this mystery of cows and men conducted
by the slender stalk of grass I held in my hand.

My uncle roused me by jiggling a wire
just inside the fence with his wooden cane.
Go ahead, he urged, your straw will reach.

I heard the snap, then felt an electric
jaw unhinge itself and strike. My uncle
laughed until my aunt called us in to lunch.

Karen Glenn

CHIMERA

This morning early, I followed
the rural roads deep into Nevada,
rolling and curving through the tiny towns
until I found the place I'd read about

where some sheep have human livers,
others human blood, and just one,
a human heart. It was in your newspaper, too,
I bet, not some H.G. Wells nightmare,

filled with beasts that groan and speak,
but a lab farm, scoured and neat,
shining with aluminum and chemicals,
a place where a liver grown

inside a sheep is not a horror, but a hope
for folks who need one. At first
it was a disappointment. In the lab and
in the field, the sheep crowded together,

baaing—looking, acting just like sheep—
nothing distinguishing about them.
But then the one with the human heart
followed the scientist who'd made him

with his eyes, watched the tracks
her small feet made across
the lab's damp floor. He stood stock still
in the stall when she touched him

with her cold instruments, then nuzzled

her soft hands. Even I could feel it.
It's something we all know—
how the heart keeps wanting, wanting

the unnamable, the impossible, yearning in the dark,
like a sheep at night in a cold barn.

First published in North American Review.

Richard Newman

MOWING

Sitting quietly, doing nothing,
Spring comes, and the grass grows by itself.
—classic Zen poem from the *Zenrin Kushu*

I'm no Buddhist, but I know enough of lawns
to say the grass grows by itself even
when I'm not sitting quietly. Take now,
for example: I'm in a terrible mood, full
of so much desire and April cruelty
I could wash away the four noble truths,
and, almost as I mow, the new growth
pushes against my chloroplasted shoes.
Even as a child visiting Virginia,
I gazed down picnic-perfect battlefields
and guessed that before the last cannonballs
burst and the last dying soldiers cried
their mothers' names into the air, the grass
was already swarming back up the bloody hills,
as it now goes about its green business
with entrepreneurial zeal, cracking sidewalks
and dishevelling my brick patio.
And when my daughter swings in our back yard,
crying, "Watch me, Daddy! Look how high!"
I look up from the mower as she launches
into the leafy arms of the trees, the whole
swingset heaving, then swoops back down again,
her bare feet riffling over the blades,
grass I scattered with my own two fists,
and I know—sitting, standing, quiet or not—
that as she grows there's nothing I can do.

From Borrowed Towns (*Word Press, 2005*). *Originally appeared in* The Sun (*July, 2004*).

Peter Bisset

EARTH BEINGS

They don't like dry, waiting underground as patiently as the dead
The generous rains of the summer thunderstorms
They pop out of the ground like they are late for a date
Pushing the dirt out of the way with the top of their heads
I can walk a mile or two not noticing the distance, head down, eyes glued
At feet level. The woods move around me. The human trail is gone.
      I walk in circles.

The mushrooms can be playful, one second hidden, the next
Right at the corner of the eye.
Some the size of a bongo drum, others the size of a softball
I smell and sigh, these sweet surprises, pick the firm ones
Almost sexual in shape, they rise above the earth to spread their spores.
I stuff my fanny pack, the mushrooms the colors of burgundy,
    buff, rust, red
The same colors overhead across the sky as I descend into dusk,
My cooking treasure, resting warm against my lower back.

Claudia Putnam

AFTER FLOWERS

*(For a girl shot by Chinese border guards while crossing from Tibet
to Nepal, September 30, 2006. Witnessed, videotaped, You-Tubed.)*

How vast the blossomed meadows, Kelsang Namtso.

How we love to name our daughters
after flowers.

Kelsang, lavender shade of the seventh
chakra, so close to heaven—
thriving like the edelweiss
in the high air, sipping on the snows.

Is the daughter named
for the holy lama,
        the flower for the lama,
or the lama for the sweetness,
        in the purple flower?

She was seventeen. Is it loveliness
we wish for our daughters
when we name them after flowers?

Delicacy? Daintiness? An efflorescence?
Daisy. Lily. Iris. Violet. Rose.

We must know, when we name our daughters,
        how fleeting is their beauty, how soon
                they will fall, how quickly
                        the hard seasons will come upon them.

Kelsang Namsto, you fell
      in the high snows and were left there
      by those who had to go

into their own, later autumns. We saw you snapped
      from the stalk, we saw you bleed into the headwaters.

         You were seventeen.

We saw you go.

Jan Hadwen Hubbell

CARRY ME

He turns me around the corner
Smooth as a freighter's captain
Coming to port.
And there's curry in the air
Fiery and deep
Steaming from the sidewalk.

Men in a hole
Near a store called
"The Remains of Light."
He carries me now—passed
A basket store
The reeds, assembled,
Hanging.
And me hanging on his arm
Lapping him—like the
Water laps the reeds
Before they're dried.
Hanging on his every word
The way the baskets are hanging
Carry me—
Carry my longing
Till you drop
Till the end of the dock.
To the water's edge.
Captain me—
And the moon is
Two moons across the
Water. Near the pier
A bench appears.
Carry me till our footprints

Mesh
Till our hearts break
And the water breaking in
The dawn.

Kim DeFries

LOVE FOR APPLES

and men lived to tell the tale
    of how she fell
how her love for snakes & earthly browns
    her love for apples ruby round
made her the one to blame
made her the one to hide in shame
    to cover, to maim...

    but her flesh forgotten
        the light's revealed
            spirit knows no sin

Kim Nuzzo

FIVE DREAM FRAGMENTS

1.

In the dream I'm a blind donkey
in the great raw theater. There are those
who want to bury me.

2.

The mountain is full of words
and grunts. A saint comes
along to beat me.

3.

It's nighttime and I see
my redemption in the bright grass.
She has wings.

4.

I'm eating breakfast at Denny's
with men without hearts. They
steal a bit of the morning sun.

5.

I watch the garbage man,
a thousand wounds under his tongue,
sick with his wishes.

Craig Nielson

BOTANICAL PRAISE

So I asked the double jack pine snag
Clinging to the side of the mountain
Great tree, were you the tree of knowledge?
"All trees living or otherwise, replied the pine,
Are trees of knowledge"

So I asked the shrubs and bushes
The colonies of shadows populating the land
Oh shrubs and bushes, why do you grow so broad
And with such equability?
And they answered back to me
"Something has to anchor this old earth"

So I asked the perennials
The boundless regenerators rising from
Their matted death
Perennials are you the harbingers of life?
And the perennials answered
"No, we just have to learn
When to lay low and when to rise"

So I asked the multitude of annuals
The great flourishing of color and fruit
Annuals, why must you blossom and produce
For such a short while?
And the annuals replied
"Impermanence is the nature of things"

So I asked the weeds
Proliferating by the thousands in my dry yard
Loathsome weeds, why can't we praise you
as we do the plants?
"We are plants dumb ass!" said the weeds, "praise is for fools"

Karen Day

HARD TRIP HOME

Even though apologetic prayers to God were sent
we couldn't be sure of surviving
the dark & the tornado & the winds
blowing us from Amarillo
northward towards home.

Boiling ominous black dirt
was grabbed from the cotton fields,
sifted through oil derricks &
flung against water towers with
names like
Dumas, Dalhart, Texline,
outposts en route to Colorado.

At Raton, my love laid his hand on my knee,

"You're safe now. You're with me."

Four months later I turned 'round,
headed south &
laid him in the ground.

Sterling Jim Greenwood departed April 27, 2013, at 1:30 in the morning.

Stewart S. Warren

THERE WERE DAFFODILS

"I left silence, so they could listen to themselves."
—It's Raining in Augusta, *Renée Gregorio*

Enough of the hollow house
and later episodes of debauchery.
There were daffodils in my mother's garden.

There was percale, de Haviland, Francis the First,
Tchaikovsky, Robert Lewis Stevenson.
There was a sled with soap for the runners
that belonged to my brother, for nearly
everything came to him first,
but the mittens and forehead kisses
    were my very own.
She tucked me in sober and clean.
She was my mother then.

"When you're halfway up the stairs,
you're half way down."
Mother Goose was lighter than Grimm.
We turned the pages carefully,
magnolias filling summer rooms.

Through open windows, always
a little hammering, some tapping
from a neighbor's shed, a saw
on a bench set in a yard, the yawn of a cat,
the dull ring of stones stacked and fitted.
The noon whistle!

The world was round then: refrigerators,
curve of the hood and trunk, mirror

in the parlor, phonograph records, father's fedora.
Things came around on a regular basis:
bootleggers, Saturday mornings,
valentines, milkmen, tetanus shots.
I'd wake her with a marigold.

I drove the tricycle all by myself.
     I was quiet as a mouse.
I was sitting on the floor humming
in a bar of golden light.
I was recording all this.

Rett Harper

A MOTHER'S WISH

When I held my newborn son in my arms
I thought of making wishes, invoking charms.
I was full of mother love and proud,
but the only thing I said aloud
was "I hope I can dance with you on your wedding day."
That was really all I wanted to say.

The twenty-eight years of raising a son
clouded the memory of that first incantation.
On October 2nd the wedding came to pass.
The mother and groom dance came at last.
It was more than I ever hoped for,
as we twirled and swirled on that grand dance floor.
I've nothing more to ask, now my dream has come true.
Oh…well…maybe a grandchild or two.

David Mason

S H E   I S

a small wolf eating a caul

a girl holding the leg
of a broken doll

a true egg
fertilized by a swan

warm gold in the water
but a cold dawn

after the slaughter

a hurt tune
lying still in a dark room

a knapsack crammed with words
unpacked

repacked
like a deck of cards

a sine curve
in a line of thought

all nerve
uncaught

First published in Kin.

Cameron Scott

DOG EARTH

for Scout

We've abandoned the world
of tap water and cell phone coverage

for cold rivulets of snow-melt
coursing through corn lilies
and skunk cabbage,

the rasp and scrape of rose hips,
clatter of rocks down scree fields

and still I cannot make sense
of this great void between dog
and man, it is as if we were hunting

always teetering between instinct
and domestication, but only one of us

ever notices what lies hidden
in the underbrush before

leaping into the green
and disappearing.

Claudia Putnam

EXCAVATED

I thought I would read of Pompeii
one year after my visit there. All that pumice
crunching underfoot. Deadly.

And then I slipped off to dream of you
unexpectedly. I always thought of you
as Mediterranean,

pictured you bounding down cypress
hillsides on some Greek island,
your fine-lashed eyes faunlike. Lovely.

It's hard to trace the dream threads
connecting lives. You looked sexy—
your hair longer, a little more weight.

Curse those archeologists,
romancers of what was meant to be
obliterated. Utterly.

First published in Tar Wolf Review.

David Rothman
ONE SOLUTION

After the woodchuck
Had chucked
All the wood
That he could—
Which wasn't much,
For though we did instruct
The woodchuck
In how he should
Chuck wood,
He was no good—
In fact, he sucked—
We found that if we duct-
Taped the wood
To
The woodchuck
And then threw
The woodchuck
With the wood
We could construct
A serious stack
Of wood.

Though, boy,
Have I got to tell you
That that woodchuck
Did not enjoy
Being duct-
Taped, repeatedly hucked,
And then,
Again
And again,

Being untaped, plucked
Up from the wood
With which he had been chucked,
And carried back
To the remaining
Pile of wood.

Jimi Bernath

AT THE MUNICIPAL FARMS

At the Municipal Farms I met my love,
hoeing weeds in a beanfield with a blue sky above.
Our eyes met as we both mopped our brows.
From a nearby pasture, the lowing of cows
made us smile, and those smiles were bright
in young tanned faces living in the light.
We leaned our hoes on an old beanpole,
a long drink of water was the very next goal,
so we smiled and drew from our Camelbacks
letting our arms and shoulders relax.
"I'm Ben," I said into eyes of green,
hoping to narrow the distance between.
She told me, kind of shyly, her name was Rose
(as indeed it still is, heaven knows).
She came nearer, we made small talk
while glancing at the flight of a distant hawk
who turned eastward and headed our way,
as if he'd just thought of something to say.
He flew in circles right overhead
and as we looked up at him, a voice in me said,
"What sky and soil have joined this day..."
and then we had some more weeds to slay
before our shift in the field was over,
but that very night we began to discover
the common ground our hearts would sow
and cultivate, so our city-tribe could grow
with children and food fresh from the land,
in partnership with a divine loving hand.
We've retired now and are still well fed.
Our children and theirs work the land instead.
A cooperative world will long endure,
and I never really saw it, till the day I met her.

Lawton Eddy

SONNET FOR MY LOVE

In light of day 'tis plain we are well matched
both drawn to simple beauty and the truth
That we can both entwine and yet detach
a measure of our wisdom gained—post youth

The tune I start your whistling completes
your visions, your designs I clearly grasp
Our melding forms in sleep beneath the sheets
the ease with which we've joined suggests, perhaps

The mystery which does and will not cease
to manifest pure thought into a form
has worked again through us its masterpiece
unspoken though it is, we've duly sworn

to handle with great care this fledgling bird
Love, which, in the beginning, was the word

Previously published in Colorado Central.

Kim DeFries

THE SLIPPING SANDS

The morning in its mystery
               held still for sunrise
quiet in holding a memory of where its been
              and why it's back
to grace a face with color
               to fill our hands with the slipping sands

my body an hourglass, turned over again
        each day, every grain giving birth to the next…

        moment of gratitude

Cameron Scott

THE GULL

I can't help but nod
to the rough shadowed hulk
of a man and his

Doberman. Starts me flapping
around women who ignore me
and children who hide

behind legs. Suddenly I jump
sideways from an odd couple
who split apart on the sidewalk

last second. Mom, every year
I'm more like you. Make small talk
with cooks who throw fries

as the human world closes
over me like a fist, everywhere
concrete and strung wires,

compelled to sleep on doorsteps,
wrapped in wings,
one eye open for cats.

Barbara Ford

EXPLORATION

Once, he planted his private flag
on the slope of her breast
claiming ownership of the mole

discovered there—
a miniature brown hillock
on which he built a tiny hut

to use for rest and refuge
during midnight wanderings
over the pale landscape of her skin.

Later, they lost each other
as young lovers will
called by other voices

other places. Occasionally
what remains of his small shelter
appears in the morning mirror—

vast sweep of sky showing
through the thatch, birds' nests
balanced on rafters

flag shredded by the storms
that visit every woman's breast
as she climbs and descends
climbs and descends.

Patrick Curry

AFTER BEING IN LOVE

You remember the joy of your bodies
touching, exploring, exposing
opening, cavorting, drenching
pressing in endless clutch, oh, the joy
you remember the morning coffee chats
with Sunday news, over Eggs Benedict
giggling, laughing, discussing the darkest movies
lying politicians, untimely war, how to save the world

You don't remember the moment
without discussion, when your bodies
were no longer interesting, news was bad
coffee cold, conversation stalled, eyes averted
as love slinked down the front steps
out into the street in search of the next body

Don McIver

DAMEN STOP

A rickety ride
on the Blue Line to Bucktown.
Snow falling on the city as we grind up the self-imposed hill
as the train goes from subway to elevated
and the city opens up down below both windows:
small wooden decks with neglected grills,
graffiti only a commuter will see
and no eye contact,
headphones,
small quiet conversations,
people concentrating on books
as each stop is announced
and suddenly it's Damen—my stop.

Platform made of steel,
covered in creaky weathered wood
with grey snow pushed up into corners
and the crowd steps off the train into weather,
windy, wet, wintry weather
and we wind our way around an equal number getting on
and we march in asyncopation,
bottled up behind a big, lumbering black woman,
carrying too many bags to make these slip-steel steps
something navigated haphazardly.
She slips...
and the air from the rush hour commuters withdraw in
        one long, uniform gasp.
No one,
no one steps around or over,
even people down below her stop and crane their necks to check-in.
"Are you okay?"

comes a muted question from someone on the Damen stairs.
She mumbles, then lumbers up,
with the help of some stranger as he helps her down the steps.

Chicago…Carl Sandburg calls you the "City of Big Shoulders,"
and today you showed me why.

Craig Nielson
BIRTHDAY ON THE FREMONT

Birthday on the Fremont
fifty years riding the big orb
around the sun

It's warm in the desert
the muddy river
murmuring its gravity song

It's good to sink
your feet in the sand
to sit amid the strata of rock
and consider your
epigrammatic account

It's good to witness
the river's passing
and the breeze cueing
the yellow cottonwoods
to perform their fractal shimmy

It takes more than a day
to reconcile a life
but a day is more than enough
time to find the stillness

Come evening
I loosed the dogs
from their Ziploc kennel
for a final swim down the river

their powdered carbon
suspended above the ripples
like some holy shroud
ashes to ashes, dogs to dust

After the final light
fades from the canyon
It's time to rise from the bank
and welcome the fire's heat

After a passage in the mystery
it's good to grab onto the handle
for another turn

David Rothman

MARIPOSA LILY,
CALOCHORTUS GUNNISONII

Emily said they were out above the caves,
Thousands of them in this delicious spring
When the rains returned, and so I went to see,
Up Cement Creek, then left on Walrod,
Left again on the single-track into that high meadow.
I was seeking with my hungry eye
My favorite flower, rare and then abundant
Briefly o so briefly in these mountains:
Three big, bright white petals in a tight cup
Standing on a long, green slender stem,
Like a grass with a bomb on top.
A broad band of neon yellow fuzz fringes
An elliptically shaped glandular structure
Near the base of each petal,
All of it framing the stamens,
Their elegant tripartite purple sex.
But I had waited too long,
Stormy monsoon afternoons, work,
Chores, children, life intervening,
And that great hillside was already drifting,
Despite soaker rains, into its summer fading,
Grasses heavy with seed and tall,
The fields of sunflowers rustling, petals gone,
Dry, already turning back towards sleep.
A few dozen laggard lilies still stood here and there,
The ten thousand others gone as if they never existed,
Perhaps another seven years until they return like that.
And I missed it, my favorite flower, I was late,
So that now like ancient children alone in their cave,
Muttering in their hunger to try to appease it

By making the sounds that they would make if eating,
If only there were food, if only there were food,
Until that inarticulate moaning rose into words
And became prayers and paintings of the hunt,
I can only sit and say again and again,
As I gaze into a fire stoked with clocks:
Mariposa Lily, Mariposa Lily, Mariposa Lily.

Previously published in The Gunnison Valley Journal 9 *(2010)*.

Claudia Putnam

THE QUEEN GAZES INTO
THE MIRROR, BEHOLDS

These scars on my belly from my son,
I own them.
The one on my cheek, where the branch

pierced me when the horse
threw me,
I own that.

The smile lines circling my eyes
I can take those.

But these on my forehead from worrying
about my son's heart breaking
when his father broke mine,

the creases from the job I had to take,
which was wrong,
which made me sleepless,
which took me far from what I loved,

why do I see them
as beauty-killers?

Why can I not brag about them
and the gray hair too,

as I do the mark of the horse,
the broken leg from skiing,
and all the other
battle scars?

David Feela

TRADITIONAL VIEW

Veils of virga over the Ute Mountain
like gauzy curtains on the horizon,
like half-formed dreams billowing
in one corner of the Four Corners.

Powwow drums of thunder,
lightning sharp enough to bead
the rain, a zigzag pattern against
the shawl of this sleeping earth.

Barbara Reese

CIRCLES

In that time
in late August
when the sky reddens
with the setting sun
and the air is heavy
with remembered rain,
barn swallows begin
their daily practice.

Circling in
lazy patterns
over the pool,
one by one
they dip down
until the V of each beak
barely breaks
the water's surface
forming circles
flowing out and out and out;
an old Victrola needle
playing a watery surface.

Then, in statued lines
twenty, thirty, more
wait atop a whitewashed fence
for some silent signal.
Rising as one
they float
up and out and back;
a perfect C
to be repeated

over and over
and over
until the purple
dusk descends.

Year after year
I have been their witness.

Ron Byers

MANGROVES ON
WOMAN KEY

Said she was going to take me
To an island of man groves
To see what would happen
When the tide went out
Could we live on the strange things
In the brackish water
Or would we eat each other
Would I demand to see a menu
Could I grow into a singing chorus reef
Could I lure my loved ones
To explore the wreckage of me
She said to wear my Life-jacket
To always buckle up
Was it the her-eye-cane of he
Or the he-eye-cane of her
That finally washed us away

Jolie Ramo

EARLY WINTER/INDIAN SUMMER

Indian Summer.
The late afternoon
Stretching the road
In front of me

Low clouding. Lingering fog...
Then on cue as in the theatre
Late Sun
Drenched bright.
Fields refreshed. Clearing skies.

Under the white mist...
Unrolling in front of me
A clean blue mirror
Shining the sky
On a dark black carpet
Of rolled-out wet light

Then, high-gloss clouds
Whitening the black mirror—shiny-slick:
The sky bluing the
Road.

Glancing tall winter grasses topped with
Late-lit snowflakes, bird-like, delicate
High-bright
Balancing on the
Reeds—Alert.

Crystal stillness.
Awake fields in their first snow
Stolen cadence.
Late sun. Silent road.

Ron Pike

THE GETTING OF WISDOM

All growth is a spontaneous leap in the dark;
An unpremeditated act, sometimes for a lark.
Fearlessly let intuition be your guide.
Develop the strength to swim 'gainst the tide.
For courage like muscle is strengthened by use.
Be not subdued by verbal abuse.
Skeptical searching is the path to being wise,
Mind always open and so to your eyes,
To history and science and so to subsume,
The nurturing of thoughts and never assume,
That personal beliefs are so sacrosanct.
That reason and truth are somehow outranked.

WHO ARE THESE PEOPLE? (BIOGRAPHIES)

ROGER ADAMS is news director for Aspen Public Radio (KAJX/KCJX) and has worked as a public radio reporter since 1982 in Florida, Michigan and Wyoming. He grew up in the Panama Canal Zone and currently resides in Basalt, Colorado. He earned a degree in anthropology from the University of Southern Florida. Adams wrote his first poem in 2007 having been inspired by the work of Raymond Carver and having studied under the former Poet Laureate of Wyoming, David Romtvedt.

JOSÉ ALCANTARA teaches math in Glenwood Springs, Colorado. He started writing poetry four years ago after a quasi-mystical experience in a graveyard involving Dante, a dead woman named Guadalupe, melting frost, a raven and some church bells. He is the recipient of a 2013 Fishtrap Fellowship in Poetry.

JIMI BERNATH has been on the Denver poetry scene for over 35 years and has been featured in numerous readings and performances. His poems and other writings have been published in national and international journals and anthologies. For the last 20+ years he has concentrated on haiku as a primary form of expression and spiritual practice. Jimi has taught classes on haiku and renga at Colorado Free University and facilitated workshops at The Festival of the Imagination and elsewhere.

PETER BISSET lives somewhere considered out of bounds, better known as the Back Side (of Aspen Mountain). He pads his nest with words, and he is comforted by them. He has no desire for fame or success with his poetry. He is soothed when face to face with other poets across the room at Live Poetry Night. "I will be forgotten and it doesn't bother me. The words will live on in the bottom of boxes."

CHARLES BRADDY is a lifelong resident of Colorado. For the past 25 years, he has been a resident of the Roaring Fork Valley. His poems are snapshots of life, places and characters he sees every day.

SUZANNE BRONSON is the author of *Passion Play*, Mestiza Press, Los Angeles, and *The Keeper of Days*, Farolito Press, Colorado. A long standing member of the Aspen Poets' Society, her poetry has also appeared in *Grand Valley Magazine, Colorado Journeys, Colorado Life*, the *Aspen Daily News* and *The Daily Sentinel*.

RON BYERS lives near Viroqua, Wisconsin, and has worked as a photographer for decades. He writes quirky, satirical, sassy-surreal dark humor poetry, often looking at the Divine Fool aspects of human nature. Ron also hosts a radio program exploring the dynamic realms of word-play and music collaboration.

ED CROSS grew up in the eastern suburbs of Sydney, Australia. Following a ski trip to Thredbo in 1965, his passion for the sport of skiing eventually led to Aspen, Colorado. Ed worked on the Aspen Mountain Ski Patrol from 1971 to 1988. He began writing poetry in 1971 and credits the Aspen Poets' Society with a renewed interest in writing new poems and the cataloging of many of his early poems. Ed has poems in *The Ski Book* and Hunter Thompson's *Kingdom of Fear* as well as many submissions to Aspen newspapers.

LOGAN CROSS was born in Aspen, Colorado, and grew up enjoying reading and creative writing. Her father's interest in poetry inspired her to develop her natural talents.

PATRICK CURRY currently resides in Carbondale, Colorado, where he spends most of his time growing start-up technology and marketing companies. When he isn't triple-tasking on his multiple devices, he wanders the streets looking for poems. From time to time he finds one. He is an open mic reader at local poetry venues. The highlight of his poetry life was reading as a featured poet in the 2013 Karen Chamberlain Poetry Festival.

KAREN DAY, an interior designer, grew up in the Texas oil camps around Midland and Odessa. She and her journalist husband, the late Sterling Jim Greenwood, also from West Texas, "uncontinuously published" the *Aspen Free Press*, a hand-delivered newspaper which, beginning in 1982, proclaimed itself to be "Aspen's worst newspaper."

KIM DEFRIES is somewhat of a closet poet, not a prolific writer, but when she does allow herself to read, write or listen to poetry, she immediately feels that sense of coming home: being so at peace in heart and soul, she knows it's where she instinctively belongs. "The creative call, too often unacknowledged, can bring one to tears at how healing it is for all of us."

MARJORIE DELUCA moved to Aspen in 1974 after obtaining a degree in creative writing/journalism, and moved to Carbondale, Colorado, a few years ago. She renewed her interest in poetry in a workshop with Cam Scott; she is a member of the board of Aspen Poets' Society. Her poems have been heard on radio stations KDNK and KAJX, and appeared in a local newspaper. (And that's all she wrote.)

SANDRA DEXTER first wrote poetry and haikus in second grade and loved it. But, alas, that was very short-lived. Her next stab at poetry was a half-dozen poems in 1994 for a class. In 2008, she began journaling daily and poems started to show up unexpectedly. The poetry continues to come through sporadically. She looks forward to a time of words flowing freely in the form of splendid poetry and prose. The thrill is superb whenever a poem shows up.

SANDRA DORR grew up in the lake country of Minnesota where she dreamt of mountains. After many migrations, and three adventurous children, she landed in Western Colorado's canyons, where she dreams of water. *Desert Water* (Lithic Press, 2009) may soon be followed by a novel, *Girl in the Sea*.

LAWTON EDDY's writing history began with childhood diaries, rhyming poems, love letters and stories. Recent adventures with poetry include publication in *The Mountain Gazette, Colorado Central* and collected works by The River City Nomads, a poetry troupe with which she performs. Lawton lives, loves, works and writes in Salida, Colorado.

DAVID FEELA's work has appeared in regional, national and international publications. He was a contributing editor and columnist for eleven years at *Inside/Outside Southwest* magazine. His chapbook, *Thought Experiments*, won the Southwest Poets series, his first full-length poetry collection, *The Home Atlas*, was published by WordTech Editions and his most recent book, *How Delicate These Arches*, was selected as a finalist for the Colorado Book Award.

BARBARA FORD lives in Poncha Springs, Colorado, where she offers her poems to the crosswinds of two mountain passes. She uses her weekly show on community radio station KHEN to spread the gospel of poetry. Recent poems have appeared in *So It Goes*, Volume 2, and *Transnational Literature*.

MICAH FRANZ is a 23-year-old conscious individual, poet/writer, chef, naturalist, minimalist, existentialist, and vagabond who believes positive pollution is the easiest way to corrupt an institution. He is a native Earthling who loves the arts and outdoors. Micah has hopes to travel the world to share dreams of love, peace and revolution.

CATHERINE GARLAND has lived in the Roaring Fork Valley all her adult life and every day she falls more in love with its mountains, its valleys, its weather moods, its people. Writing is her passion. The first "book" she wrote was at the age of six. It was the story of a Gypsy family and was illustrated by her mother. Writing poetry is what comes most naturally to her, though she also enjoys writing memoir pieces and short stories.

KAREN GLENN is the author of the poetry book, *Night Shift*. She read the title poem on NPR's *All Things Considered*. Her poems have appeared in *Poetry Northwest, Chattahoochie Review, Denver Quarterly, North American Review* (which nominated her for a Pushcart Prize) and many others.

ART GOODTIMES of Norwood, Colorado, poet, deep ecologist and Rainbow Family elder, weaves baskets, grows potatoes and is Colorado's only Green Party county commissioner. He is the founder of Talking Gourds and has been responsible for poetry events since 1989. From 2011 through 2013, Art served as Poet Laureate of the Western Slope. His most recent book is *Looking South to Lone Cone* (Western Eye Press, 2013)

RETT HARPER holds an M.A. from George Washington University. She has been writing and directing children's plays in the valley for 30 years as well as teaching English and theater at the high school and junior high school levels. She has taught public speaking at CMC since 1993 and has a private "coaching for public speaking" practice. She is vice president of the Aspen Poets' Society and reads one of her new poems each month at Live Poetry Night.

VALERIE HAUGEN is associate artistic director of Thunder River Theatre Company in Carbondale, Colorado. In 2012 she published a book of poetry, *Naked Underneath*, inspired by the firm belief that poetry saves lives. Haugen also organizes the annual Karen Chamberlain Poetry Festival which takes place at Thunder River Theatre the last weekend in March.

JAN HADWEN HUBBELL studied writing with Pulitzer Prize–winner Bernard Malamud at Bennington College. She earned an MFA in fiction writing at the Iowa Writers Workshop. After ten years as a writer on Wall Street, she began another career as an English professor. Currently, she is writing screenplays, one of which won five awards at various film festivals. She has won two Academy of American Poets Awards for her poetry.

LAURIE JAMES was born during a blizzard to a one-eyed man and a one-thumbed woman. Her inspirations flow from the great western landscapes she travels. Born and raised in Montana, she is now a 42-year resident of Salida, Colorado, where she spins her metaphors in view of a lone pine and the wide-open sky. She also performs poetry around the state with the five-member poet troupe River Ciity Nomads.

LYNDA LA ROCCA is a freelance writer and poet who lives in Twin Lakes, Colorado, and performs throughout Colorado with The River City Nomads, a five-member performance-poetry troupe founded in 2004. Her poetry books include *The Stillness Between* (2009, Pudding House Publications, Ohio) and *Spiral* (2012, Liquid Light Press, Colorado).

KATHLEEN MARIS's poems have appeared in *ILK, Alice Blue Review, Thrush Poetry Journal, In Digest, Sugar Mule Literary Magazine, Sun's Skeleton,* and *Poems by Sunday.* She recently completed her MFA at the University of New Hampshire where she now teaches.

DAVID MASON is the Poet Laureate of Colorado and has written and edited numerous books, including *Ludlow: A Verse Novel, Sea Salt: Poems of a Decade,* and *The Scarlet Libretto.* More of his work can be found in *The New Yorker, The New York Times, Poetry, The Hudson Review, The Wall Street Journal, The Times Literary Supplement, The Threepenny Review,* etc. He teaches at Colorado College.

ERICA MASSENDER, a student from Carbondale, Colorado, found her passion for poetry under the influence of poet and visiting teacher Logan Phillips. Erica wrote her first poem, *Shadow Girl,* when she was 12 years old. She read it at a poetry jam in a competition with high school students and took first place. At age 13, she continues to write poetry in addition to working on three novels that she aims to publish one day. Erica hopes to pass her passion for writing onto others.

MARILYN MCDONALD, poet, teacher, artist, started life in a small Canadian town, moving to Denver as a child, seeing life through the eyes of a poet. Writing at an early age gave her a way to express and bear joys and struggles. She is determined to build good and to smile, because it feels good.

DON MCIVER, a resident of Albuquerque, New Mexico, is a slam poet, an award-winning radio host/producer, writer, editor, rhetor and monologist who's published widely and performed all over the United States. Visit donmciver.blogspot.com for more of his writing.

RICHARD NEWMAN is the author of several poetry collections, including *Borrowed Towns* (Word Press, 2005), *Domestic Fugues* (Steel Toe Press, 2009), and the forthcoming *All the Wasted Beauty in the World.* His work has appeared in many periodicals and anthologies including *Best American Poetry, Boulevard, The Sun,* and many others. He lives in St. Louis where he plays in his band, The CharFlies, and edits *River Styx.*

CRAIG NIELSON is the founding member of the poetry troupe The River City Nomads. He is the author of the collection *Touch of Grace,* and the forthcoming collection *Three Houses.* His poetry and prose have been published in *Pilgrimage Magazine, Mountain Gazette,* and two regional anthologies. Craig lives in Salida, Colorado.

KIM NUZZO is a Roaring Fork Valley performance poet/actor. He is president of the Aspen Poets' Society and a host/co-founder of Live Poetry Night at Victoria's Espresso and Wine Bar in Aspen. You can read his poems on his blog, Aspen Holyfunk, at www.heartofeverything.blogspot.com or on Facebook.

HEIDI OWEN has written poetry in the mountains of Montana and Colorado and beside the ocean in Alaska. She currently lives in the north woods of Minnesota with her husband, Scott.

RON PIKE, known as "Pikey" to most, also refers to himself as the "Bushy from the back of Barellan." As a child, he listened to poetry in a humble family farmhouse located on the dry plains of the Riverina in Australia. Now retired from irrigation farming, Ron has more time to write poetry and comment, often related to the environment in which he grew up and worked most of his life.

SARAH PLETTS was born dancing. As a young woman, she performed with the Miami Ballet and soon embraced modern dance, painting, poetry, and film. For Sarah, watching and listening in dark theatres, studying a work of art, or reading alone on a comfy couch are places of wonder.

CLAUDIA PUTNAM grew up in New Hampshire but has raised her son in Colorado. After 30 years in Boulder, she now lives on the Western Slope. Her fiction and poetry appear in many literary journals. A chapbook, *Wild Thing in Our Known World*, is available from Finishing Line Press. Her awards and residencies include the George Bennett Fellowship at Phillips Exeter Academy, which gave her a year away from her job to work on both a novel and a poetry manuscript.

JOLIE RAMO, writer, editor, creative director and film producer started a media company called Sonic Images in Washington, DC, in 1980 that grew to 60 employees by 1993. Jolie is a dancer, yogi, T'ai Chi Chuan and Pa Kua artist. As Jolie states, "Poetry clarifies the mind of its habits, opening depths of fun…and the shallows of intrigue…"

DAVID ROMTVEDT grew up in an Anglo-Chicano community in Arizona, then college in Oregon, Iowa, Texas, Peace Corps in central Africa, carpentering in Nicaragua, Olympic Peninsula, Southeast Alaska, now at home in Buffalo, Wyoming, writing, playing music and teaching one semester a year at the University of Wyoming.

DANNY ROSEN runs the Lithic Press. A Pisces, he lives with three dogs and a dolphin in the desert of Western Colorado. His next book, *History of the Universe: a short poem*, will be out soon.

DAVID J. ROTHMAN published two volumes of poetry in 2013, *Part of the Darkness* (Entasis Press) and *The Book of Catapults* (White Violet Press). That year he also published a collection of essays, *Living the Life: Tales from America's Mountains & Ski Towns* (Counundrum Press). He serves as director of the Poetry Concentration in the low-residency MFA program in Creative Writing at Western State Colorado University and teaches at the University of Colorado, Boulder. He is Poet in Residence for Colorado Public Radio.

CAMERON SCOTT has been an editor, contributing editor and edited contributor to various magazines and literary journals. His first collection of poems, *The Book of Ocho*, was recently published (AGS Publishing, 2013).

DAVID TEITLER has published countless (or at least a couple of) articles in prestigious publications (*The Crested Butte Chronicle*, *The Valley Journal*) and now his poetry can be seen in timeless anthologies like the one in your hands.

CATHLEEN TREACY wrote her first poem in sixth grade (she has a copy of it somewhere) and has been hooked on words ever since. Instead of taking photos, she has always memorized the moments in her life with verse.

ROSEMERRY WAHTOLA TROMMER's poetry has appeared in *O Magazine*, in back alleys, on *A Prairie Home Companion* and in her children's lunch boxes. Her most recent collection is *The Less I Hold*. She is a parent educator for Parents as Teachers. Favorite one-word mantra: Adjust.

STEWART S. WARREN is a writer, evocateur and catalyst for positive community. His poetry is both personal and transpersonal with a mystic under current. Stewart is the owner of Mercury Heart-Link, a small press in northern New Mexico, and is the founder of the Albuquerque Poet Laureate Program. www.heartlink.com

INDEX

By Author

ASPENPOETS'SOCIETY, INK

The Aspen Poets' Society, Ink, is a grassroots 501(c)(3) non-profit organization founded in 2006 by Lisa Max Zimet and Kim Nuzzo. They recognized that there was no singular organization in Aspen solely dedicated to promoting and supporting original poetry and to providing a consistent venue for the spoken word to be heard.

Since its inception, the Aspen Poets' Society has sponsored and hosted Live Poetry Night, a monthly gathering for all poets and listeners—locals and visitors alike—to share the poetry of musicians, open mic participants and featured poets, all on a voluntary basis.

For nearly five years, poems written by Aspen Poets' Society participants have appeared weekly in the *Aspen Daily News'* "Poets Corner" in a continuing effort to keep poetry alive.

Now in its eighth year, the Aspen Poets' Society has expanded its reach throughout the Roaring Fork Valley and beyond with goals of promoting poetry related activities in local schools, collaborating with other literary organizations and partnering with other art groups.

One hundred percent of the proceeds from the sale of *A Democracy of Poets* will be used to further the activities of and ensure the continued viability of the Aspen Poets' Society. We thank you for your support.

CPSIA information can be obtained
at www.ICGtesting.com
Printed in the USA
BVHW081350250521
608098BV00007B/1665